Pigeon

Pigeon

Karen Solie

poems

A

ANANSI

This edition published in 2009 by
House of Anansi Press Inc.
110 Spadina Avenue, Suite 801
Toronto, ON, M5V 2K4
Tel. 416-363-4343
Fax 416-363-1017
www.anansi.ca

Distributed in Canada by
HarperCollins Canada Ltd.
1995 Markham Road
Scarborough, ON, M1B 5M8
Toll free tel. 1-800-387-0117

Distributed in the United States by
Publishers Group West
1700 Fourth Street
Berkeley, CA 94710
Toll free tel. 1-800-788-3123

House of Anansi Press is committed to protecting our natural environment.
As part of our efforts, this book is printed on paper that contains 100%
post-consumer recycled fibres, is acid-free, and is processed chlorine-free.

13 12 11 10 09   1 2 3 4 5

LIBRARY AND ARCHIVES CANADA CATALOGUING IN PUBLICATION

Solie, Karen, 1966–
Pigeon / Karen Solie.

Poems.
ISBN 978-0-88784-823-0

I. Title.

PS8587.O4183P53 2009   C811'.54   C2008-907522-6

Library of Congress Control Number: 2008941439

Cover design: Bill Douglas at The Bang
Text design and typesetting: Ingrid Paulson

 Canada Council   Conseil des Arts
for the Arts   du Canada    ONTARIO ARTS COUNCIL
CONSEIL DES ARTS DE L'ONTARIO

We acknowledge for their financial support of our publishing program
the Canada Council for the Arts, the Ontario Arts Council, and the Government of Canada
through the Book Publishing Industry Development Program (BPIDP).

Printed and bound in Canada

For David

Contents

I

Pathology of the Senses
—*July, 2005*

Oligotrophic: of lakes and rivers. The heat
an inanimate slur, wool gathering, hanging
like a bad suit. Suspended fine particulate

matter. And an eight-million-dollar ferry shoves off
for Rochester, no souls aboard. I see you,
you know, idling like a limousine through the old

neighbourhoods, your tinted windows. In what
they call "the mind's eye." Catch me here
in real time, if that's the term for it. We work our

drinks under threat of a general brownout.
Phospholipase is activated by bitter stimuli.
Back home, we call this a beer parlour.

I washed my hair at 4 a.m., he says. *The full moon,
it was wack.* He can't sleep. The woman
who says *pardon my French*, over and over,

can't sleep. They are drunk as young corn. Sweet,
white, freestone peaches. A bit stepped-on.
You said we'd have fun. Do I look happy?

Our fingers, our ankles, swell in unison. Word
spreads. "Toronto," in Huron, means
"place of meetings." Even now, you may be

darkening my door. *On my bike*, she says, *I dress
all reflective*. Even now, you're troubling
my windbreak. The vertebrate heart muscle

does not fatigue and is under the regulation
of nerves. I'll wait. First it's unlike evening. Then
it's unlike night. Thirty degrees in a false

high noon, no shade when all things lie
in shadow. The lake a larger mind with pressures
brought to bear, wet hot headache

in the hind brain. Above it, cloud racks up.
A mean idea it's taking to, breathing
through its mouth. In this year of Our Lord

your approach shoulders in, the onset
of a chronic understanding. Rivers underfoot,
paved over. Humber, Taddle Creek,

just the way they sound. To be abyssal
is to inhabit water below 1,000 feet.
I need a good costume, he says, *but don't

know what that entails*. Walk the districts.
Misery of heritage buildings. Superheated
rooms of the poor. Sorry, cooling station

closed. Lack of funding. I like my feet
covered up at night, doesn't everyone.
Blinking, naked atop our sheets. Smoke

rises but won't disperse. Air hairy as a fly.
In fly weather. Tight under the arms.
It also depletes your spinal fluid. In your spine.

Aesthetic injury level the degree of pest
abundance above which control measures
should be taken. God, what she's wearing.

I'm tolerably certain you know the way. Red
tide of the sidewalks. Pass the dry cleaners
. and Wigs, Wigs, Wigs! It used to be called

100% Human Hair. That's right. "Ontario"
an Iroquois word meaning "sparkling waters."
Like doleful seaweed, our predilections undulate.

Rats come out to sniff garbage blooms
in rat weather. Heavy cloud, colour of slag
and tailings, green light gathering

like an angry jelly. Pardon my French. The city
on rails, grinding toward a wreck the lake
cooks up. When you arrive, you may

be soaked to the skin. A tall drink of water. Darken
my door. *All of my organs are fully involved.*
He's a little freshet breeze. We are as any microbes

inhabiting extreme environments, surviving
in free-living or parasitic modes. Chins above
the germ line. Is it true a rat can spring a latch.

Is it true all creatures love their children. Raccoons
and skunks smell society in decline. That sag
at the middle. Rat weather. Fly weather. A certain

absence of tenderness. Who will you believe.
Bear me away to a motel by the highway. I like
a nice motel by the highway, an in-ground pool.

It's a take it or leave it type deal. Eutrophic:
of lakes and rivers. *See now, she says,*
that's the whole reason you can't sit up

on the railing, so you don't fall over. Freon,
exhaust, iron motes of dry lightning. *Getting*
pushed, he says, is not falling. Jangling metal

in pockets, you walk balanced in your noise,
breath a beam. I harbour ill will. By this
shall you know me. Caducous:

not persistent. Of sepals, falling off
as a flower opens. Of stipules, falling off as leaves
unfold. Speak of the devil, the devil appears.

Wild Horses

The Iberian head, roman-nosed. Black,
bay, chestnut, dun, some buckskins, palaminos,
roans, a few paints, stouthearted, with primitive
dorsal stripe, *equus callabus* returned
to the New World in the sixteenth century
as Spanish Andaluz mustangs, blessed with speed,
a good fear, their ears' ten muscles. Only a dog's
nose is keener. Escapees of expansion
from Mexico, their descendants, travelled north along
the Rockies, millions coast to the Great Plains
restored to the authority of the herd, its shelter,
its law, knowing from birth which rivers
they can cross, where sweet water lies,
and the saltgrass. In wolf scent, winter hunger,
deerflies, rear blindspot. Points of balance triangulate
from the skull, behind the shoulders. Jaws
can snap a coyote's spine, hooves halve rattlers.
Before twentieth-century machinery they fell
ahead of ranchers and oilmen, cleared
from coalfields staked at Bighorn, the survey's
immovable starting point in rocks above the falls.
From ridges travelled summer and winter,
they were driven into passes and corralled.
A few hundred remain on grizzly lands below
hanging glaciers, among Engelmann spruce, fir,
lodgepole pine, foothills of aspen and balsam poplar
in the Siffleur, White Goat and Peace Wilderness
where they're shot for sport, caught for rodeo stock,

sold for dog food at four hundred a head. Sixteen
left to rot in the forest northwest of Jasper,
two foals dumped at a gas well site by the only
animal who kills from a distance, noise for a voice
and noise for a home, for whom all places are alike.

The Girls

They stayed at home. They didn't go far.
Trends do not move them.
From picture windows of family homes

they cast wide gazes of manifest pragmatism:
hopeful and competent, boundlessly integrated,
fearless, enviable, eternal.

Vegas, Florida, Mexico, Florida, Vegas.
With children they travel backroads
in first and last light to ball fields

and arenas of the Dominion.
We have no children. We don't own,
but rent successively, relentlessly,

to no real end. The high-school reunion
was a disaster. Our husbands got wasted
and fought one another, then with an equanimity

we secretly despised, made up over
anthem rock, rye and water.
Our grudges are prehistoric and literal.

It seems they will survive us. The girls
share a table, each pitying the others their looks,
their men, their clothes, their lives.

Bone Creek

We planned to camp in a remote valley
among the hills at the east end of X.
It satisfied all our prerequisites—
shade trees, a trout stream, some vague
narrative significance. Rumours
involving Sitting Bull feature
in the literature. Those days, in the city,
we squabbled like geese, cursing
squalls of compounded heat until,
steadily, you assumed an expression
that described a wide arc around
our situation, and I yearned
for the peaceful life that happens
in the country. Next,
we learned from my cousins of a disturbing
incident. That Y, a man from nearby Z,
a washed-up town with a bad
reputation, made a nuisance of himself
to people camping in our valley.
Cheap beer, threats, the usual.
That this, among other things, is what
he's known for. The exact nature
of all of it remains unclear. Once again
we were visited with a grave doubt.
That night I dreamt I drove to Z.
Found Y beside a two-toned brown Sierra
Classic parked outside a plank bar.

I watched him as the hawk watches
the hare. Considered him, neighbour
to neighbour, the way one king
considers another. First I shot out his tires
and then I shot him. And that
was the end of that. I woke to everything
as I'd left it, but later, a morning lit
by the tail lights of summer
and the weekend edition face down
in the yard, swollen with dew,
general interest, product reviews
and more news of the wars.

Wager

Off-season brings rain and new life
to old habits. Whatever it is that we're doing, we can't help
wanting to. Roadside attractions of the great southwest
are nothing without us. The World's Largest animals,
vegetables, minerals, fade and fall over as junk
beside our beloved minor highways, and the Four Aces
in Kingman, Arizona, having suffered the attentions
of the Board of Health, has closed its doors
for good. I'm telling you,
if you believe it's worse never to have tried,
then you haven't really tried.

Though the evidence confirms a deeply unimaginative
lack of decent judgement, it's possible,
in the echoey solitude that is resolve's aftermath,
to venture out into the hour of diminishing contrast,
under cautionary perfumes of the chocolate bar factory,
with the intent to do no harm. The honourable life
is like timing. One might not have the talent for it.
Take this guy up ahead who's driven 45 minutes
with his turn signal on through this jurisdiction of few exits,
as if the hope of a left is all he's got now
in his one chance on this earth.

The March West

The Redcoats brought their law
to the borderlands and lawlessness
with it. From the two, local economies
were born, these dead towns
that make the maps wrong now,
barely a ruin at a crossroads
to mark their passing, deserted
in the ageless prospect. To drive
the trail is to go unremarked on, a criminal
with a small window of opportunity
in the anonymous glory
of the itinerate moment. It's terrible,
what a person can think up,
and want.
            This is where
optical illusion was invented.
Light stands on the coteau like a herd
of antelope, and deer scare
from where no deer were.
Where all is visible, so all
may vanish.
            Men lost during
the march west, when recovered,
spoke of God's eyes on them
as the earth and its creatures
turned their faces away. In the distance,
death rattling, broad in the rims,

no weakness of luxury to it.
Must there always be something
for which we are prepared
to lose everything?

                        Regret has many
offices. But the motel
furniture is placidly ahistorical,
and on the bed, a fabric
of uncertain provenance. Here,
one might swear, as days wind down
around the campfire of the television,
that mistakes of the past
shall not be repeated. And as night
lays a hand on each numbered door
in turn, listen to constellations advance
on the foothills. To that first machine:
a wheel, and an axle, and a rope.

The Prime Minister

He looks out to the spring night composing its indifferent themes.
He looks out through his point of view. Looks through

the window to the darkness, which throws him back. He stares
at the night, his mirrored face, as into an unsolved

private sea. His pain elusive, dangerous, vastly intelligent.
Like the largest living giant squid his pain down there in his private sea.

He reflects on the playoffs, the anthem sung by a sellout crowd
at Scotiabank Place, dead soldiers' faces scrolling through TV time-outs,

and starts to weep. Afterwards, he is simply starving.
The way a good cry can really make a person ravenous.

II

Four Factories

1.

At the nominal limits of Edmonton, refineries wreathed
in their emissions, huge and lit up as headquarters
or the lead planet in a system, as the past
with its machinery exposed—
filters, compressors, conveyors, you name it—
basement upon basement upon basement.
Around them gather opportune spinoffs, low-slung
by-product support outfits named in functional
shorthand. *Altec*, *Softcom*, *Norcan*, *Cancore*,
subsidiaries crawling onto the farmland.
Employees are legion, transient,
and union, turning what happened before we existed
into something we can use, at capacity
day and night. As we sleep, they build our future.
Which, as the signs say, belongs to all of us, is now.

2.

Worth leaving the highway for. Gorgeous
at sunset, really outstanding,
the potato chip factory at the east end

of Taber, which is a kind of town.
It's painted a bright and not entirely baffling
turquoise, for who would want

their snacks to issue from a dour scene?
Crowding the parking lot's acre of slab,
against evening's mauves, pinks, blues

and tangerines, it looks like a monument
to grad night in the midwest
or a wedding after-party at the Holiday Inn.

There's a nicotine tinge to the white concoction
frothing from the stack. In the morning
it's work, an okay wage, metal door

of the employees' entrance ugly
and dented forever, yesterday's effluent
still fizzing in the drainage pool.

3.

The global appeal of concrete is not accidental.
Through it, our modern vision is realized. That "cement"
and "concrete" are used interchangeably
is one of the most interesting things about it.
This confusion is rooted deeply in our language.
West of Dead Man's Flats, at Exshaw, they make
cement. Pre-eminent in the limestone gap, the plant
appears to describe its situation accurately, reflected
in the lake that cools the wastewater.
Scenery north of Heart Mountain goes vague
in kiln dust from the clinkers.

Pity the diatoms, first to go, trout eggs
choked by sediment in gravelly streambeds,
ducks in chloride runoff. Pity us,
we're all messed up about it. Nearby are the old
company towns. Kananaskis and its lime plant.
Seebe's power dam has closed. But in concrete
is an ancient technology ushered into
the 21st century: in condos, dude ranches,
four-season resorts, the demand for improved
infrastructure and amenities in the recreational
community of Lac des Arc.

4.

In cold, the blood smell clangs. In heat,
      flies observe it. A functional non-
architecture's slaughter capacity.
      We're coming back to Newfoundland

with our mobile recruiting team!
      No experience necessary. High school
not necessary. Must be willing
      to work with a razor-sharp knife. Revised

prison recruitment strategies. E. Coli.
      Recalls. Must tolerate extreme heat
and cold. Bandidos in town on a recruitment
      initiative. RAID. Burgeoning drug

trade. Brooks' Chamber of Commerce
        welcomes your input. Delusive, debilitating,
awe-inspiring tedium. *I Heart Alberta*
        Beef. Team members should expect

heavy physical labour and fast-paced
        repetitive tasks. Team members
should expect to be called team members.
        The killing floor. Caricatures of supervisory

misconduct. Unprecedented growth. Labour
        unrest. A crew of managerial thugs
mobilized from Arkansas. The Canadian
        Forces steps up its recruitment

campaign. Our industry's future remains
        secure. Additional openings in rendering
and hides. Animals are not our friends. Sign
        on the highway, *Always, 100 Jobs!*

Air Show

The up-there
shredded, hanging
in flystrip with our nerves

stuck on it. Screw us,
we're in turnaround
airspace. Down here

fuel costs rise 15
cents overnight.
C-130 Hercules, C-140

Aurora, C-17 Globemaster, C-18
Hornet, F-16 Viper, T-38 Talon
Celebrating Freedom

Through Flight, celebrating
car alarms, panic attacks, canine
episodes, migraines,

childhood hearing loss,
and it's free, an added bonus
of the CNE. The last word

in military aviation
technology. The last word
in everything

for those paying now,
right now,
for the real show.

Bow River Preludes

I

Cloud, a great skein of it, drawn through the eastern eye
of the Bow Valley by a frontal hook, rolls over
the foothills, purls up thick above the ranchlands. Material
of autumn's visible ceiling. The river nourished by glaciers
in their last weeks of melt at the tail end of the long
20th century. Perking at the falls, it reconciles south
along the golf course to its downstream designation:
the best trophy trout destination in North America.
Tour buses come and go, everyone suitably amazed,
looking as if they've arrived set at the wrong speed.

II

The river is laden with suspended
particles of finely powdered
rockflour. All colours
of the light spectrum are absorbed
but for what these particles
reflect. A frozen mineral green.
Tug at the loose thread under
the heart green, the green that does
nothing of the kind. How dare you.
It teems. It is a measure
of our limits. The green here
and not here at once, that sets

our ears to ringing. Moss, geode,
iris green. Green pins
of cold and cuts of thirst,
relieved. Now do you know where
you are? That green. An orientation
to which the mind returns.

III

The river is older than the mountains folding
in heaves around it. From here, everything follows
eastward in rational or irrational
arrangement. Warmed by ingredients, fibrous,
acquiring odours of its passage, it mingles
with the Oldman and the Red Deer at the feet
of cities, arrives at the muddy basin of the South
Saskatchewan looking inward and browned, its eyes
lowered. By this time, many lives will have changed.

Tractor

More than a storey high and twice that long,
it looks igneous, the Buhler Versatile 2360,
possessed of the ecology of some hellacious
minor island on which options
are now standard. Cresting the sections
in a corona part dirt, part heat, it appears
risen full-blown from our deeper needs,
aspiring its turbo-cooled air, articulated
and fully compatible. What used to take a week
it does in a day on approximately
a half-mile to the gallon. It cost one hundred
fifty grand. We hope to own it outright by 2017.
Few things wrought by human hands
are more sublime than the Buhler Versatile 2360.

Across the road, a crew erects the floodlit
derricks of a Texan outfit whose presumptions
are consistently vindicated.
The ancient sea bed will be fractured to 1000 feet
by pressuring through a pipe literal tons
of a fluid—the constituents of which
are best left out of this—
to tap the sweet gas where it lies like the side
our bread is buttered on. The earth shakes
terribly then, dear Houston, dear parent
corporation, with its re-broken dead and freshly
killed, the air concussive, cardiac, irregular.
It silences the arguments of every living thing
and our minds in that time are not entirely elsewhere.

But I was speaking of the Buhler Versatile 2360
Phase D! And how well recognized it is
among the classics: Wagner,
Steiger, International Harvester, John Deere, Case,
Minneapolis-Moline, Oliver, White, Allis-Chalmers,
Massey Ferguson, Ford, Rite, Rome.
One could say it manifests fate, forged
like a pearl around the grit of centuries. That,
in a sense, it's always been with us,
the diesel smell of a foregone conclusion.
In times of doubt, we cast our eyes
upon the Buhler Versatile 2360
and are comforted. And when it breaks down, or thinks
itself in gear and won't, for our own good, start,
it takes a guy out from the city at 60 bucks an hour
plus travel and parts, to fix it.

In New Brunswick

Daylight fails crucially along the St. John River
and a focal point of damp sand
dims. Suddenly, like a junked mattress, a tire,

in the flashlight of the immediate future
one is come upon. The forest,
with its long hallways and concealing furnitures,
is not for me.

One hundred yards from the highway
is primeval in its ferns and muck and drowned
hardwoods below the floodline.
Cellular turnover is practically audible.

I'm in the middle of my life. I see it
as through a crowd, from a bad angle,
and the show continues.

My industry fails me. The first person fails me
utterly, again and again, like a landlord.
Even the flakeboard plant rusting vividly
in coastal fog is more than the sum
of its glues and dodgy management.

On the far shore, trees
in inestimable numbers grey as one
toward evening, sleep standing like horses
in thin smoke of the fires up at Minto.

The World of Plants

In the world of plants, there is no Airbus 380.
Yet they're reborn to us selflessly
in fossil fuels! People, we're at the centre
of a great mystery. Last night saw us
dragging through the clubs, their soggy
double-digit martinis and vocals that reek
of auto-tune, suspecting someone else's fun
was having us. We snuck back through
the hole in the wall that's the door
to the part of the house that we rent
and re-entered the good life—
innocence of the new-mown grass blades,
our neighbour who clears his piece of sidewalk
with a hose, endlessly,
while the available portfolio
of non-prescription medication expands softly
as the evening around us. Circling,
a red-tailed hawk pinpoints the moving detail
of his meal in the big picture. We love him
from afar. Soon, we will have to have him.

Our longing hovers like billboards
over the expressway, the same questions,
same answers, throughout each long night.
The lake accumulates what is given it,
until gradually, though it may not appear so,
its constitution is changed. One thing dies,
another takes its place, and an unknown
potential enters the world. Anyone
who spots the alien invader Asian
longhorned beetle in the neighbourhoods
is asked to report this immediately
to the city. Without our efforts, no tree is safe.
It's as if everybody always wants us to do something.
I'd like to see someone make us. Please,
someone, come on over here and make us.

Cave Bear

The longer dead, the more expensive.
Extinction adds value.
Value appreciates.
This may demonstrate a complex cultural mechanism
but in any case, buyers get interested.
And nothing's worth anything without the buyers.
No one knows that better
than the United Mine Workers of America.

A hired team catalogued the skeleton,
took it from its cave to put on the open market.
Retail bought it, flew it over to reassemble
and sell again. Imagine him
foraging low Croatian mountains in the Pleistocene
and now he's flying. Now propped at an aggressive posture
in the foyer of a tourist shop in the Canadian Rockies
and going for roughly forty.

The pit extends its undivided attention.
When the gas ignited off the slant at Hillcrest
Old Level One, 93 years ago
June, they were carried out by the hundreds,
alive or dead, the bratticemen, carpenters,
timbermen, rope-riders, hoistmen,
labourers, miners, all but me, Sidney Bainbridge,
the one man never found.

Pigeon

Synchronicity is a theme
science can't explain. Mutual
appreciation brought us
no closer. More like
we showed each other what we're
made of. The human brain,
three pounds soaking wet,
its attentions divided.
My attentions were divided.
Nevertheless, I saw what I saw.

Archive

Though it appears in the photograph as fog, snow is falling in its fractal specifics straight down onto the city. The day is calm. Light appears as though filtered through a white sheet. The disposable camera is unable to register the snowfall's particulars, its slight woozy drift as a bird flies through it, and in fact the photographer isn't very good at taking pictures. It's difficult to capture falling snow in a photograph. Sometimes, against the headlights of a parked car at night, it can be done.

The calm day is also warm, a break in a long brilliant wire of low pressure along which sound had travelled from great distances, engines and cries rendered proximate. Falling snow dampens resonance. The morning is the body of a different instrument.

The photographer has chosen a disposable camera due to a fear of heights. She must cross the High Level Bridge to get to where she works, and this is easier some days than others. On an afternoon of strong winds, nearing the bridge's midpoint, handled roughly, simultaneously by updraft and downdraft, she recalls a childhood event: she and her younger sister riding bikes on the dirt road perimeter of a dying hamlet where the family lived in summer while grasshoppers ate paint off the walls. Her sister had offered that if they got tired halfway, they could always turn around and go back.

But in its calm and warm, its falling snow, this day is so beautiful that the photographer's fear is lessened a little, and she wants a picture of the river to look at later. A document to locate her for people far away. The photograph is shot from the middle of the bridge looking east, though it feels to the photographer, somehow, south. The white shape in the bottom left corner is her hand on the rail. Uneasiness requires that she hold it tightly while lifting the camera to her eye. Because the camera was not expensive she feels that should it fall for some reason the 50-odd metres to the river, she will not have lost something important.

In this way, her fear and where it comes from are also in the photograph. As is the snow melting on her hair and shoulders, falling behind her and farther until it reorganizes as another system. As is traffic's rumble and clank at her back, groggy spirals of exhaust that don't do anything for the nerves. Supported on the diagonal by girders, the concrete sidewalk overhangs the bridge's steel struts, hangs right out there above the valley. The photographer admits that her faith in the long-term success of human ingenuity is limited.

The first train crossed the bridge in 1913, an occasion celebrated by the shrieking of many whistles and sirens. Its 8,000 tons of steel, 500,000 cubic feet of concrete and 1.4 million rivets cost 2 million dollars. The economy was different then, but not so different. Workers earned 35 cents an hour. One man died in a cave-in. Three others fell. The bridge is 13 metres wide and 755, 775, 777, or 877 metres long, depending on who's measuring and how. In winter it loses a half-metre due to the contraction of metals.

There are animals in the photograph — squirrels, rabbits, deer, foxes — though they are unseen, and fish down there, presumably. She's heard that immersion in the North Saskatchewan raises welts on human skin. Sour gas ventures are popular in the area and there are various categories of runoff. At the east end of a short stretch of open water, ice shelves up like wrecked drywall of a huge house. That tiny smudge to the right of it is a bohemian waxwing in flight, is possibly a bohemian waxwing. The water is greener than it appears and moving fast. Crawling over itself and under the ice again. Pressure on the bridge supports is calculable and enormous.

The photographer lives in an apartment hotel housing short- and long-term tenants who have nothing in common except that they live in the building: oil patch and construction workers, hospital outpatients, students, retirees, professional football players, clients of addiction and mental health services, overnighters, and those whose temporary situations have gone long-term. There's a bar on the ground floor. Once in a while, Deb the bartender turns every one of its seven televisions to a cable channel that seasonally devotes itself to a looped shot of burning logs until Bill, a resident and regular, waves his arms in mock panic and yells at Deb to switch stations. "It feels like my goddamn house is burning down," he says, and everybody laughs. The photographer learns from Deb that Bill moved into the building after his house burned down. "And now he's been here five years," she says fondly. "Wrong again," says Bill. "Four years, six months, two weeks, and three days."

What is seen is true, as seen, though may be interpreted falsely. The photographer's read that the mind fills in dimensions of a viewed object based on the experience of objects of its kind. That, often, we believe in things we see the same way we believe in things we don't. She looks out over the valley, wondering if it makes any difference. She's overdressed. Snow falls onto her face, her hands, her neck where she's loosened her collar and scarf. The air feels carbonated. She slides the plastic camera into her coat pocket and walks the remaining half of the bridge, though there are a few pictures left on the roll, a decision which is in the photograph. It explains why this one instead of, possibly, another.

The camera remains in her pocket for days afterward, the ice, moving water, falling snow, white hand gripping the bridge rail and bird in flight recorded there, the light of their going-on latent in darkness. Like how, in the photograph, incipient leaf buds stir inside stark branches of poplars along the river. An image which does and does not exist. It's during this week that a university student kills herself by jumping off the bridge. People say bloodstains are visible on the ice, though it's reported shortly afterward that flowers have been thrown there. The paper issues a warning to stay off the river, as the ice is no longer safe.

Atoms move at an infinite speed. By virtue of their weight, they tend downward. Allowed to behave naturally, they would fall vertically and uniformly and would never meet.

The photographer leaves work, begins the walk home. What was the end of the bridge is now the start. She steps out onto the first part with air underneath, past a yellow sign warning that the deck is slippery during waterfall operations. On special summer days, the city pumps tons of fresh treated water up through pipes and over the east side of the bridge into the river. Then everyone takes photographs. It's the world's first man-made waterfall, 7.3 metres higher than Niagara Falls, and called The Great Divide. Once, it was activated on New Year's Eve. Water blew across the road alongside the river and froze inches thick, causing many crashes and editorials concerning the dumb ideas of paid officials.

It's colder now, and dark. The photographer walks carefully, flatfooted, with short strides, because the sidewalk has frosted over. Wind throws snow from all directions in a heavy biting mist. Holding her scarf and collar closed at her throat, she remembers standing on the patio of a Niagara tourist facility, soaked in spray, watching slabs of spring ice hang at the green lip of the drop as though, in that moment, something else were possible.

In December, 1874, hotel owners in Niagara Falls purchased an old Great Lakes schooner and advertised a spectacle they called "The Reverse Noah's Ark" to lure the curious in low season. After loading the boat with a buffalo, three bears, two foxes, a raccoon, a dog, a cat, and four geese, they sent it over the falls for the appreciation of those assembled, who were then further enticed with drink and accommodation. One version has the geese survive. Another claims the cat was found on shore, eyeless, with broken legs, and that for years entrepreneurs maimed cats to sell to tourists. No one seems to know if any of this is true. But neither does there appear to be anyone who believes it could not have happened.

The photographer is less frightened crossing the bridge at night. Imminent threats of proportion are diminished. She feels the immediacy of walking in known conditions and her thoughts radiating through the abstracted landscape. There is no visible dangerous middle ground.

Having achieved the north side, once through the poorly lit legislative grounds with its eternal flame, the photographer uses a scan card to unlock her building and rides the shaky elevator

11 floors to her rooms. She hates the elevator, but has decided it would be stupid to avoid it and encounter a heart attack in the stairwell. It's dark by 4 p.m. She lies in bed listening to the endless track of traffic around the apartments and condominiums where residents sleep stacked into the sky, and considers how a person can get used to almost anything.

Though the city reflects dimly off the slice of open water, the valley is very dark. It contains the day and what went on in it though now everything has changed. Light of the coming day is also there. Nothing springs from nothing, and nothing is ever destroyed.

At least twice a month, when the fire alarm goes off in the photographer's building, everyone mills about the lobby uselessly like participants in a cruise disaster. She's told that, the year before, someone's homemade bomb exploded, accidentally, on the fourth floor. A woman leapt from her window into the arms of some football players and was saved, but a man on the other side of the building jumped alone and died. "Three storeys and you've got terminal velocity," says a fellow tenant in camouflage pyjamas. "Three storeys and you might as well jump off the top of the World Trade Center."

In the mid-'90s, the bridge was subject to extensive rehabilitation. Flaking lead paint was removed and 100,000 litres of a friendlier kind applied. Girders for the Pratt and Warren truss spans were welded, fitted, and original rivets replaced by bolts. It was discovered that some segments had lost fifty percent of their mass to corrosion. Of the men who died in the bridge's initial construction, one remains entombed in the north pier.

What does it mean, Wittgenstein asks, that hair can look blond in a black-and-white photograph? Does it indeed "look" blond, or do we conclude that it is? Because the word "blond" sounds blond, he says, it's even easier for hair to appear so. *It would be very natural for me to describe the photograph in these words: 'a man with dark hair and a boy with combed-back blond hair are standing by a machine.'*

The end of contemplative attention is a purity of heart. Sometimes after work the photographer sits by the window in the bar watching motorists expertly negotiate the icy, snow-covered 105th Street hill. Someone has been murdering women in the city. One is found stuffed under a motel bed, one in a hockey bag, one in a wooded area, and another on the edge of a golf course. On television, a police spokesman delivers a possible profile. The killer likely drives a high-mileage half-ton or SUV with a large toolbox in the back. He may enjoy fishing, hunting, camping, off-roading. He might have to drive long distances for his job. He could have been seen washing his truck at odd hours. Rob, who is staying in the building, says "that pretty much takes care of every guy in here." Rob left his wife up in Fort McMurray and is deciding whether to go back. "She's not the woman I married," he says.

Four days after the golf course victim is found, people walking in the valley see a body on a large piece of ice floating toward the bridge. Police go out in boats to retrieve her. They guess she is between 12 and 20 years old.

What we can know is defined by what we can't the way a being is clarified by the elements that sustain it. At last measurement, the Columbia Icefield covered 325 square kilometres. The river originates there, 1,800 metres above sea level at the Continental

Divide, flows northeast through the foothills, through aspen parkland with its paper birch and river alder where hundreds of bohemian waxwings overwinter, through Kalyna Country riverland, through Saskatchewan, to Lake Winnipeg. It joins the Nelson River, empties into Hudson Bay.

The photograph appears black and white but for the muted green of open water and the brighter painted green of the low bridge to the east although red dogwood and ochre hearts of scrub are in it. In it, everything keeps happening—the snow falls, river flows, the photographer's hand holds the rail and the bird is flying. The valley bending to the north keeps bending, though snow in the photograph is water now and that water an element of another landscape. A world that is this one too. Moments before the photograph was shot, a person in a bright blue jacket walking with a yellow dog along the trail beside the river disappeared into a knot of trees, moving like someone with a backstory. They can't have gotten far.

All this is in the photograph. It is and it isn't.

III

Erie

A trip to the Erie shore on the cheap side
of shoulder season, to a working port

and low-rent summer beach resort
for local 18 to 25ers home

from school. The ice cream stands, tourist
shops were mostly boarded over, a few

dopey dance clubs padlocked, flyers
for wet t-shirt contests and quarter shooters

scattered like headlines after a war
through what might be called downtown.

The lake was brown, rolling in a cold wind
from Michigan, a shallow subconscious

dredging itself up, hooked on nitrogen
from phosphorus runoff, still dreaming

of fire on the Cuyahoga River, that felonious
tributary intruding at Cleveland.

We would read later of a dead zone
in the central Erie basin, but were happy

then, the bay exhaling in damp algal
gusts as we walked beside it.

. . .

Erie's memory is going, invasive species
at its mind from the inside, spreading

like a desert. Up on farmland, between drying
sheds, harvested fields of cash crops,

switchgrass, alfalfa, and lakeward
stands of hardwoods, we passed a sign

for a cottage rental, *Erie Breezes*....
Our plans had yet to emerge. It was a golden

age of all things being equal. On Hawk
Hill's muddy cliff, we shivered an hour

before a single raptor shot over water
west to east — it was late in the year —

but from the road at a stone's throw,
two harriers hovering as if on strings

above the market of verdant margins
gone to seed. We got our cameras out,

then argued about your choice of music
all the way to Port Burwell, where, over

the long view, we agreed to disagree,
as gravity corrects a standing wave.

. . .

Perch burgers, perch and chips, all-you-
can-eat perch buffet, Sunday supper

special: perch. We ate perch cheeks
at a family restaurant in which smoking,

active or passive, was unofficially
mandatory, located as it was on the outer

ring of influence from Tillsonburg,
then drove on through country of scant

middle ground — grim mansions
of unprincipled dimensions and small

structurally iffy houses whose junk fell
over itself joyfully down the creekbanks.

At the wind farm, minimalist daisies
rotated on humming vertiginous stalks,

chunks of air like bathtubs falling
around us, good intentions complicated

by avian mortality and the eternal
complaints of The People. Nothing's

perfect, I said, trying to please you. I didn't.
But that's okay, you said, that's okay.

Double

It's lucky to have someone to talk with.
To whom this strange soft snow falling
out of the blue, for example, might be
described, that thought defined,
and the past, always, its fortune,
hellish stopovers, sheer marvels
of bad planning, affection. Likewise
to listen, doubled within and without
against sorrow's long compromise. What

is this remainder, then—selfish,
inconsolable—setting out alone
each night to wander freeways' dangerous
collectors, amid hanging gardens
of electrical transformers, through
the so-called green belt's terrified
remnants, sustaining a truth that can't
be spoken, from like place to like place,
never giving the same name twice?

Medicine Hat Calgary One-Way

The bus is a wreck, and passengers
respect that, a mild unease aboard
this have-not province
with its per-capita demographic representation
of unfortunates, poor earners, procrastinators,
the criminal element, hammering away
at the dullest stretch of highway
on earth. Local industrial calamities,
unmistakeable turquoise PVC of the deadly prairie
waterslide, tractor-trailers, poorly tied
private loads, all of it
ill-used and ugly in early spring,
though bright hawks balance on warming
updrafts, and a young sun tosses its jewelry across
tabletops of Ducks Unlimited wetlands
fed by a late snow. Your lives are neither
before nor behind you. In the limitless
present of schedule 0063, you embrace
secret multitudes. Suffield, Brooks, Gleichen,
Bassano, Strathmore, taking on
packages, grey water of smoke
breaks, in eyeshot now of the Purcell Range
and into subdivisions named, it seems,
out of malice, grief, or confusion, and perfunctorily
treed. Walk-in closets and walk-
out basements march forth in staggered
plans. Oldies stations. Man-made
lakes. Strip malls and big box stores whose

faces regard with solemn appreciation
the shifting congress of late-model vehicles
that attends them. Skyline
sunk in a brown fog. The zoo. *Dow Chemical
Corp. is devoted to fostering community
leadership.* Downtown deserted as the coda
to biological disaster. Then
the purgatorial boredom
of the Greyhound depot. Beige food, beer
in cans, between a Toyota
dealership and nowhere you'd want
to walk. As you leave with your bags,
hire a taxi for the airport, is it not possible
to look with love upon your fellow travellers?
Theirs is the infinite patience born of reliance
on mass transit. They wear
the arrows of their circumstance
like Saint Sebastian. Night's mountain passes,
hallucinatory tundra, its aches,
dark thoughts, anticipations
belong to them, queueing at the steel door
to the brutal asphyxiant garage. You've been
often in this company, together
resembling survivors of an apartment fire, or,
despite the odd hidden flask, children, carrying pillows
before you, a destination to live up to
in the only way you can afford.

Casa Mendoza

On public transit, I rode to meet him in the lounge
      of an old motel on a busy through-road
            in east Etobicoke, south of the Nabisco factory
      and water treatment plant amid sports bars,
tarp shops, dealerships, and self-
      storage, one of a strip doomed by the geologic
            headway of condominiums aspiring to Miami
      or Neo-Deco via Vegas. CCTV and gated
courtyards, lakeside. I was committed
      to change. Lingered in the parking lot and thought it oddly
            gracious, appropriate, private, with its rear

      views of The Beach and Silver Moon, both earmarked
for demolition, disused antennas upholstered
      in birds and the big oaks throwing their overcoats
            over everything: weeds
flowering in vacant lots, heaved sidewalk
from which I'd just seen a pair of Scooby-Doo
      underpants, men's, size XXL, in the gutter. Nearby,
            the Hillcrest and North American, in hourly
      throes of cost-to-profit ratios, were going down
in a blaze of filmic neon. The dark little lobby
      was Spanish-themed, with something German

about it, and anachronistically panelled. I was out
of my depth. Running hot and cold. From the patio
overlooking the water, the city core
appeared as background and setting
for what we were mixed up in. Even then,
a Demonstration Centre had cropped up on the long
lawn, pink to orange in the failing light like a patient,
worsening, a woman inside manning
the phones. Above that, little brown bats,
though they flew in dwindling numbers, flew nonetheless.
We knew it couldn't last, and then it did.

The Ex-Lovers

They are ongoing, in mid-season. They have mathematical
implications. A frenzy of unsustainable practice
hung a residue in the atmosphere, as though
the affairs had burned coal in their heyday,
then went abruptly bankrupt. It got quiet.
Eons passed. They re-emerged with the gravity
of unearthed figures from the Bronze Age. Now,
honestly, they've never looked better.

We're all beginning to feel mildly historic, walking
arm in arm with our former selves through streets
that look noirish and literary, as desirable properties
gain on the not-so-desirable, and a civil
population minds its peace. Sometimes a moment
acutely revisited leaves us unable
to breathe. They could do that. How unkind
it all seems to us now, and how marvellous.

Migration
—*for Cathy*

Snow is falling, snagging its points on frayed
surfaces. There's lightning
over Lake Ontario, Erie. In the great central
cities, debt accumulates along baseboards
like hair. Many things were good
while they lasted. Long dance halls
of neighbourhoods under the trees,
the qualified fellow-feeling no less genuine
for it. West are silent frozen fields and wheels
of wind. In the north, frost is measured
in vertical feet, and you sleep sitting because it hurts
less. It's not winter for long. In April
shall the tax collector flower forth, and language
upend its papers looking for an entry adequate
to the sliced smell of budding
poplars. The sausage man will contrive
once more to block the sidewalk with his truck,
and though it's illegal to idle one's engine
for more than three minutes, every one of us will idle
like hell. After all that's happened. We're all
that's left. In fall, the Arctic tern will fly
12,500 miles to Antarctica as it did every year
you were alive. It navigates by the sun and stars.
It tracks the earth's magnetic fields
sensitively as a compass needle and lives
on what it finds. I don't understand it either.

Franklin

The half-ton stalled halfway up the boundary road and would not
turn over. He lifted the hood to shorted wire and night adjacent.
South, the town on the old rail spur, a mile nearer as the crow flies
than the number two highway, a slog through crown lands of
                                                    chattering birch
and firs frozen as wind had cocked them. There were streetlights,
yardlights, visible. He set out over the crackling verge, low wind
viperish, hissing through last year's foxtails and brome and flicking
little tongues of grainy snow up from the crust. Hauling scars
of 60-odd years, he felt the breach of a subtle limit. The verge of dark
was blue and short and he broached grazing lands in the moon's
owly light, blown air in a glittering twist as the risen wind pulled
over him its blanket of stings. No discernible rabbit or fox. He followed
fencewire and phone line to their brittle limits, cocked an eye right-angled
to the boundary road and knew he had lost the truck. That this
was his life now, feet numb in the beds of their good boots. He was
a younger man in his mind. When the branch snapped from the clattering
birch, it lit up his nerves like a bone spur. Still, as the crow flies,
were town lights visible. He hove up under a fir and stuck
as wind pulled over him his blanket of snow. He met the country
on the terms of its bitter limits. Sheltered in the underbranches until
he disappeared. As the rabbit enters the owl's night eye, and disappears.

Possibly, Therefore

Let B represent the class of all registered voters.
Suppose the coin is warped toward heads.
Though disagreement and vagueness are different issues,
they may be represented in much the same way.

Conclusions congregate at the outskirts
like angry villagers, looking drawn.

Still, in the wee hours, even as the city resumes
its aerial application of Foray 48B in spite of protests,
I recall that the General Law of Likelihood does not propose
that likelihoods are always defined, and my hope returns.

IV

Prayers for the Sick

I'd thought there would be more of us. Considering
the size of the neighbourhood, its habits,
and that just generally a person hears things.
The medical staff look on average barely legal
and it seems final I'm on the other side
of that now. I wait, bearing water in a paper cone
and a vapour of mild surprise in my heart.
It wears off as the ibuprofen does,
like falling very, very slowly down a flight
of concrete stairs, O Lord, you who cast low
and raise up also, and I empathize with the guy
in the bloody sleeve who stands every ten minutes
to yell down the hall and receive a straight answer
from nobody. But there's one old man
who's badly off and at least we're not him.
He's settled into his pain like a house on poor land.
He looks out at us from the middle of it.

Doors open to rooms quieter and worse.
In some, new forms of heartbreak are being born.
Above the photocopied and laminated Prayers for the Sick,
a television on a floating shelf shows highlights every half
an hour, until a criticism erupts from among
our number so imaginative, heartfelt, and so profane
that all turn to the screen. To Alex Rodriguez,
variously at play in the ballparks of America.
Someone else saw that game, his dirty trick on our rookie.
Others, his obvious notices of contempt, and by the time

the loop repeats our eyes are some dozen-odd sets
of damnation's headlamps zeroing in
on Alex Rodriguez with an old-timey murderous wrath,
and we pray, Dear God, who heals according
to your goodness, in this time of the wild card race,
send a million goats to the Island of Manhattan,
to trouble the walls of old Yankee Stadium,
whose days, as we know, are numbered. Hear us,
who are lame non-starters. Who've seen the early-season
potential of our childhood exhausted.

Remember Ronny, who came home from a night shift
at the birdseed factory north of Lethbridge
to find his effects on the lawn of his rooming house?
He'd secured nothing in writing from his landlord,
and got it. Jesus, make haste to save us
from all those smug, nasty, overpaid, with dumb
nicknames, who would see us depart and be no more.
For the very light of our eyes is failing. Our iniquities
have overwhelmed us, and it's clear now that no one
is getting out of here by noon.

Gone are the bad old good old days. Before us,
vast unfenced acres of decline.
In this present of our enforced leisure, we consider
the record of our own bad form, the bonehead plays,
mean streaks like marblings in meat,
and it hatches in us a quiet vow
to plot our comebacks. Are we not beset
by homesickness, wayfarers like all of our fathers,

our mothers? A short span
You have made our days, only a breath.
And when we're seen to, finally, treated
with compassion, or even with civility mistaken
for compassion, sprung from emergency into the still-daylight
afternoon of one of the last decent days
of this year, for some of us it will be
with a small hope restored as we return to our positions,
to our Coffee Times or Happy Time Taverns,
cleanly bandaged, with prescriptions in hand,
still wearing our hospital wristbands.

Listening to *The Revelator*

Here is consequence, folding its wings
on the fence. Here are your chances. After years
of moving whatever you do
from one place to another in the manner
that constitutes your work, you have to admit
you know what you think. About tonight
not so much fallen as struggling to its feet, gorgeous
in spite of what it's done to you. All
is forgiven. The loneliness composed on the road, after hours,
off-shift, out of it, or left behind, the vindictive
clairvoyance of local law enforcement, protracted
incidents represented by lacunae in your resume,
strategic negotiations pursuant to the project
of getting the fuck out of there, or making
the best of being stuck where you were,
in those rooms now creaking in a forest of outlived rooms
recalled as eras are recalled, their outmoded fixtures
and period costumes, motes afloat
in parallelograms of windowlight. Who are you?
What of you persists? Your life built on intervals
the way a chord is, on changes that alter you
by thirds, by fifths, in silences the progression climbs
to where each song ends, and the next begins.

Beauty and Reality Are the Same

Sleepless hour populated
by its nightly broadcast. Shouts
from the bad strip, traffic,
raccoons at the bins, watery ring
of two shod horses on the cross street:
a half-woken sound, weighted
by officers. Remembering
how I lay awake, love,
by the Frenchman River
in the western semi-desert, listening
to coyote talk travel the coulee,
reminded of how delicately
a good gun dog will carry a shot
pheasant, to bring it in.

Meditation on Seaforth

In house dress, accompanied by toy crossbreed,
the neighbour lady tends to a surfeit of garden
engineered on the three-by-five concrete balcony
of her second-floor back unit, impatiens
and pots of cherry tomatoes reddening gamely
under squirrel wire, as residents next door, formerly
perpetrators of humanity's most unsuccessful
garage sale, insist on an incomprehensible DIY
deep into its second week. In high spirits

with heavy equipment, they're making
a mockery of my plan to ignore them in order
that I might focus alternately on details
of fore, middle, and far ground, as might a Renaissance
art critic, feeling the eye's mechanism—phone line,
chain link, north wall of the View Towers—
while buses roar around the corner like enraged bison
on the tens until half past one a.m.,
when they charge back to their principal garage
and the nose-down backhoe resembles
someone fallen asleep in a library. Households

once kept perpetual fires, ignited by coals
from a parent's hearth, banked nightly with ashes
and rekindled mornings for the life of the family
who dwelled there. The way loss burns in each day's
furnace, how the present is heated and lit by it. In 1936,
the Norris Dam near the Great Smoky Mountains

in Tennessee flooded more than four thousand
homes, some whose fires were minded continuously
for three generations under sistered beams, at the heart
of roof and plumblines. For most of us,

there will be other houses, more places we long
to return to, but don't, more loves drowned
by progress, more waking to our lives at the centre
of the universe. Through my fourteenth set of rented
windows, I observe a new racket commence on the side
street, neighbours and passers-by gathering around
a pit the idling backhoe's made. Gesturing
in five languages, they incline to it, snapping
camera phones open like croupiers in an impromptu
civic festival of what has been rediscovered.

Frontier County

Every few miles, hesitation at a crossroad.
Outside the communications network, a lone signal
circles helplessly. Our separateness among

separate things is what unites us. Swainson's hawk
aloft in his workplace, coyote hunting ditchgrass —
their unlike languages, blood at the core, each eye seeing

to its own grid. The equation allowing
the cathedral isn't the cathedral, nor is it the space
that it describes. A rainstorm from Montana

advances hours without advancing. I'm hearing
something for the last time. Our separateness
among separate things unites us: a violent wonder

at convergence. The sign on the post a map
of the area, an image shot by satellite and focussed
to where we stood in the middle, we said,

of nowhere. What I've done is not what I
might have. Every few miles, hesitation
at a crossroad. Lichen practicing infinity on the backs

of fieldstones. It's what it was before the naming
that the proper name refers to. In our separateness among
separate things we are united, the hinge

the day swings on, the hesitation, like the blind spot
between a horse's eyes his mind fills in.
In the fullness of the silence which is the silence

in the series. One of the houses in the abandoned
townsite wind blows through without stopping.

Jesus Heals the Leopard

The still small voice is wanted.
—William Cowper

A better understanding of risk may win over
opponents of incinerators in their communities.
People living next to an incinerator feel powerless to control it.
They don't enjoy having it next to them.
They can't make it go away.

Patronless and devout, William Cowper
had waited his whole life for a vision.
One night an angel appeared to him
and said: "It's all over for you."
Eight years later he completed *The Task*.

Having been asked to draw a picture
of her favourite Bible story, a little girl
turned in a paper on which a figure, recognizably
Jesus, stood next to a large spotted cat.
Which story did you choose? the teacher asked.

And if I said that Jesus was smiling and the leopard
was smiling with four toes on each foot and a bandage
on its ear, that a smiling sun shone down in rays where they stood
near a blossoming tree, and that red and blue flowers also
bloomed there, would you know what I was trying to tell you?

Dog Star

The heat is ruinous as I set out,
and the innumerable doors of the landscape
I grew up in, its fields and heady shortgrass,
remain closed to me. The news from home
is not good. Having left the husband
who for twenty years had beaten her,
having found a job and a lover,
our neighbour has died, misdiagnosed,
at 50. There is luck, and then there is luck,
and if there is any other lesson here
I will never get used to it.

So much now seems inevitable.
This small ditch fire no one stops for,
the lavish and reprehensible pop songs
of our youth, an exhausting succession
of neglected outbuildings in the rearview,
and all the great anvils thundering and sparking
along the tornado corridor west of Swift Current
in regional splendour. One home, spared,
and another, taken. There is no stopping it.
It started before we were born.

At opposing points on the horizon,
indeterminate forces are set in motion
toward coincidence, while others,
as if thrown out of sync by a minor
disruption in service, cycle outward. I arrive

and an idea assembles, as does the darkness
in the east. But it's too late.
Because once again the part of the mind
called the heart appears on the threshold,
swinging its amnesias before it like a lantern.

Geranium

It seemed needlessly cruel
that I couldn't coax even the hardiest,
homeliest, dullest of plants to grow
in the one west-facing window
of that place, with its air conditioner, sealed
with duct tape, that didn't work,
and its mouse-hole, stuffed with steel
wool, that did. And an equally
needless kindness even more
unbearable, that unexpected flowering
inside the cheap circumference
of the pot while I was nearly
bedridden, of seeds borne on a broad wind
that flew in, and volunteered.

V

Norway

I.

Perhaps it's where the child I imagined
might be found conversing fluently in several
languages. It keeps me company.
There's no harm in it.

From Bergen to Liverpool in 14-metre seas over the deep erosional
scour of the Norwegian Trench, north-south line
of an old rift valley, and the Long Forties. Then to Quebec
on the *Duchess of York A*. In a photograph,
cresting wave and painted rail before which the photographer
stood firm. At 25, she'd seen the ocean
for the last time. A train carried her into the Great Depression.
My grandfather's papers have been lost. He, too, left Kristiania—
that strange city which no one leaves before it has set its mark
upon him—Hamsun's town of beggars and thugs,
its Christian graves from the first century.

And here I am. Here we all are, who were born
in the flyover zone, landlocked,
to a vague purpose.

I am of at least two minds beside the reservoir
stocked with walleye, this sanctuary for migratory
waterfowl. The creek meanders one hundred miles
of riparian floodplain fenced for pasture. Above the dam
new lots are bulldozed, staked out, sold. Dust
rises off the road. The plan is not clear.

From the boat, the old cabin's aspect is faintly
trapezoidal, forward-leaning, its deck out
to brace it overlooking the water, to yellow hills
a scant half-mile across where there are no
architectures, not even fenceline, just large
rooms of shadow day builds in the coulee
where cattle walk. All afternoon,
Jet-Skis, Sea-Doos, whine in and out of range
like skeet. Visualize the biathlete
who drops to the trail, and, sighting,
draws tight the ragged rope of her breathing.

A late wind tows the lakebed onto shore,
the root and iron of storm through the grain.
Fields throw open their windows, crops not yet in.

Night climbs its long underground staircase.
It recalls what it has to tell us.

2.

A man visits a village outside Trondheim, asks a local
where he can buy a drink. At the far end
of the last street, says the local,
there's a path up the hill, and on top of the hill,
there's a yellow house. Okay, says the man.
Yes. That's the policeman's house.
Anywhere but there.

Persistent whaling, death metal, rate of exchange.
I know the fish in lye, the endless brine.
A particular brown cheese still haunts me.
My father brought it home for Christmas.
All its qualities preceded it. It lay
untouched, then walked off into the snow.

Oscar Wilson, a neighbour in the old days, had a wooden leg
and liked a drink from time to time. He would drive
his team to the Fox Valley bar, as our municipality
was run by bastards then, and dry. He had a good team.
On the way back he sometimes fell asleep, and King and Barney
took him home. His boys would hear the wagon
rattle into the yard, rise and bring the old man
in, put the horses up. Near Christmas,
they went out to find the leg in the wagon,
but no old man. Along the Fox Valley road, in fathoms
of drift, there he was, singing, holding his bottle of rye.
People still wonder how he managed it.

Now, snows are scarce. The land
calls to clouds in the north. Turns restlessly
under its thin blanket and dreads
the first stirrings on lower floors.

When my uncle died, the Wilson boys sat with us
in the Eagles hall through long pauses that are for some
the manner of serious talk. They became firemen
for the pension and the good union. Because
there's no question of what the work is,
and when it's finished.

Day and night, machines tended over miles in wide
open difficult spaces. The word "landscape"
burns away like a fog.
Rises like a blimp and drifts off.

Don't dwell on the past, we're told. As if
it were a plot of foul land
we could pick up and move away from.

3.

All the places I could go if my car ran.
But I have no car. Now, it seems
I have never had a car.

I lie awake in my bed like a blackout. Whether my eyes
are open or closed makes no difference, the whole
of my interior is in the dark. Darkness walks
with long strides in equal measure among the dead
and the living. I lie awake and think of a mist
like the deep sleeping breath of pines.

Traditional Hardanger fiddle music
is performed solo. The instrument has four
melodic strings, and four or more sympathetic that drone
in sustained sonorities. Rounded depths
of a booming sea and things of the air that play
upon it. There are tones between standard
intervals. Eivind Groven, a composer,
was born a century ago: *if anyone were to ask the way*
to Groven's place, they would simply be told to follow

their longing. It's east of noise and west of today's
demented tempo — just by a forest lake. And on
the other side, someone is playing.

Cypress, Elkwater, Reesor, Antelope: creekfed,
springfed lakes cloudy
as old windowglass, downcast and weedbound,
smoked with mud in the fall months. Antelope has dried
up, right through the deep part where pickerel
dove. Pushing off into autumn dusk, I would look
on campsites darkening, directly astern, and feel love
for the temporary places.

At every doorway, ere one enters,
one should spy 'round.

In half-light the cabins and trailers resemble
boats dragged up from the water, overturned.
Wood, tar, tin above, the good earth below.
All the world's obsolete antennas hum with vintage
themes, nostalgic voices. My fellow viewers,
I feel I almost know you. Our addresses trail us
like anchors. We shout a name from the bow
and it returns as silence.

4.

Soon, winter, the oldest season. Predator
and prey remain true to their natures.
I prefer a cool remove. My habits
are my own.

When pulled from the water, herring emit
a peculiar squeak and instantly
expire. They are the soul of modern meteorological
forecast. Vilhelm Frimann Koren Bjerknes
saw in their cyclonic practice the large-scale
movements of oceans and atmosphere, the cold,
warm, and stationary fronts.

Foreign scientific travels are indispensible
for anyone in our restricted situation who wishes
to develop into a man of science.

In sorrow, he left his father's house.
In sorrow did his father remain.

Stillborn twin girls, my aunts. A boy
dead at two from the cough.
"Let it sleep in a drawer until you see if it lives,"
she advised my mother, pregnant with me.

At night, atoms slow so you can walk between them
and find absence, like your old house,
where you left it. Enter, and it expands
to the size of a hotel. Its rooms
are your childhood, your work, your loves.
Everyone you know is there, all the furniture
candid, open to interpretation,
though nothing can be changed.

Something that wants to be heard
is rolling away its rock.

When it was clear we skied in the valleys, she said.
When it snowed we skied in the forests.

There is no bad weather, only
bad clothing.

Above the rooftops of megacities, aircraft begin
their descents. In the sovereign consciousness
of electrical systems, each initiatets its hydraulic
repertoire. And in each an attendant on public address:
"If this is home, then welcome home."

The Arctic Cathedral at Tromsø is glacial and geometric,
like the god who I imagine might reside there, three-
sided as any mind at Siberian latitudes
so long in twilight. Its polar nights, midnight suns.

It seems I send my thoughts out to someone on a distant shore
who doesn't exist. It keeps me company.
There's no harm in it.

The Cleaners

I knew it was past noon the way
you just know, woke from a solid, unearned
12 hours to the room's silent
treatment, sun in the position
of something swung on and missed,
and pledged myself to productivity
in my remaining days. November was grey
and December moreso, light adopting
a Scandinavian economy, but without
the social programs. There are fewer
and fewer alternatives. The sound
of a train is comforting though
the one you hear is a commuter version
whose western endpoint is Hamilton.
The night before, the 24-hour streetcar
stopped to admit a group of women
freshly off shifts in the downtown core, who spoke
in multi-accented English of spouses
and children, Christmas holidays
in Scarborough, and what hell toxic cleansers
are on shoes. Nothing had been made
cleaner because of me, no order
restored. The friend I had spent the night with
was still orphaned.

Some of these women's labours
weren't through; there was breakfast
to cook, family to see off to jobs and school,
and the washing up. As a final wave
of darkness broke on the corner, music drifted
from a bakery on the sweetness
of its work—a singer
whose songs have inspired generations
and who is a national treasure.

An Acolyte Reads *The Cloud of Unknowing*

Aspiring, not to emptiness, but to continually empty
one's self as a stream pours into a larger body
what it receives from the watershed—how midway
it carves a bed in this life, a clarity of purpose—
never ends. Simone Weil starves herself to death
again and again in London while the great mystery
appears to me as through a pinhole camera: reduced,
inverted, harmless. It's hard to concentrate, living
between Fire Station 426 and the Catholic hospital,
though the man shouting on the steps of the drop-in centre
appears, as much as anyone could, to be heroically
wrestling himself free from reality, his pain the soul's
pain in knowing it exists. I have dissolved
like an aspirin in water watching a bee walk into
the foyer of a trumpet flower, in the momentary
solace of what has nothing to do with me, brief
harmony of particulars in their separate orbits,
before returning to my name, to memory's warehouse
and fleet of specialized vehicles, the heart's
repetitive stress fractures, faulty logic, its stupid
porchlight. If virtue is love ordered and controlled,
its wild enemy has made a home in me. And if
desire injures the spirit, I am afflicted. Rehearsing
philosophy's different temperaments—sanguine, contrary,
nervous, alien—one finds a great deal to fear.
A lake-effect snowstorm bypasses the ski hills,
knocks the power out of some innocent milltown.
The world chooses for us what we can't, or won't.

Parasitology

The endangered Banff snail on its last legs
after vandals swam in its pool. Even
if they wanted to, it cannot be unswum.
A magpie flies into a pine tree, aggressively
rearranges its interior, then flaps off
like an action figure. We'll not see his kind
around here again. As though these incessant
elegies were all that is required. Days of my youth,
you never appreciated me, and now I'm gone.
Summer's turned to winter in 12 hours. Back home,
electrical storms tripped over each other
to get to us, then tore away, neighbourhoods
caught out by the sun dripping and languorous
in their undergrowth. Like the Caribbean,
he said. Which is for me yet another word
representing an unknown quantity.

Aboriginal people for generations described
this collision of valleys as a good place to meet,
but you shouldn't sleep here. So whites built
a town, a big hotel. Later, a Geomagnetic
Resonance Factor that screws up people's ions
was discovered, but by that time the gift
shops were thriving, so. That the same tourist
who approaches at this moment a bull elk
with hand outstretched, kissy noises, and face
full of camera can buy bones and teeth
of animals who lived 350 million years ago

hardly seems fair. In my dream, the far reaches
fall apart in heat shimmer, dust,
and the character of the new day emerges.

Park Place

Of all the jobs I took that summer, selling franchise coffee
in the mall food court on weekends was the worst. By noon
it would fill with transients, slackers, the mentally ill, and residents
of the seniors' complexes that ringed the commercial developments.
The place was like a terminal for the last bus out, its chairs
and tables bolted to each other, then the floor, and subtly canted
to encourage turnover. It didn't work. Morale was at an all-time low.
I'd leave smelling of burned coffee, flour, grease, and sugar,
staples of that Bible Belt city, its aggressions fuelled by resentment
and carbohydrates, citizens riveted to the drama of the new,
to the greed and disappointment of an unbeatable price, the fouled-up
orders and returned merchandise that passed for recreation.
It drove us into the streets, their constant wind, blowing grit,
offensive drivers and unwed mothers, cops in surgical gloves
bullying Natives in Galt Gardens. To nights at the Alec Arms
or Coal Banks Inn, our multiplying glasses making of the table
a fractured lens we looked through to our better selves. But when
a regular picked his friend up from the filthy rug to see him
home, and with an arm about his shoulders, aiming for the door,
drove his face into the frame so that they fell together, still
embracing, like partners in a vicious sport, we laughed with the rest,
senselessly, even as it threatened to expose the vacant hours we poured
our own lives into, that stood in for youth. I can't say we
were not happy in those days, though I didn't fully understand
what qualifies, and still don't. Already, some of our men were angry
and mean, their women secretive, adept at spin, experts engaged
in a life's work at 23. It was the way of things. Weekday mornings
I would rise, groggy but able, to minister to my allotted tract

of the ugly and architecturally famous campus wedged
into the valley of the Oldman River, to the tender and ill-suited
bedding plants I nursed through the heat-sickness of summer term.
Amid the fragrance of yellow grasses, pelicans elbowing into
the water, in my awareness of my last days in that town, I resolved,
henceforth, wherever I was, to be ready to leave without warning.

X

In the evening I go out
among the peoples of the earth,
buy a few things, and so forth.
Apartment blocks in their concrete
shoes follow me all the way
home. Nights, an infinite variety
of human experience across
forty-two channels. How can I

explain my intentions when I don't
even know how a radio works?
In the fact of your absence,
you are in some way here,
like a Beethoven sonata
or the value of x, the variable
when the outcome is unknown,
as always the outcome is unknown.

POSTSCRIPT

Postscript

Two hours on that road, and we saw no one but jackrabbits,
those innocents of plane and direction who seemed compelled
from the middle distance, magnetized to the undercarriage.
All creatures are plagued by dangerous ambiguities

that inhabit the visual realm. If approached from the east,
an old community hall at an unmarked intersection
will summon its will and say CRANDALL. From the field where
that village stood, a farmer on his mid-century Case

waved to the car as if from one of the four corners
of the known world. The first gift of any being
is that it exists. Born 50 years after Newton's death,
Carl Gauss was familiar with the angular

defect. He lived on its outsized surfaces. His beloved died
in childbirth with their newborn son, and soon after a bereft
daughter followed. Staring through his theorems, through
fearsome curves of elliptical space, he saw only the back

of his head. Random errors like a bell around a mean.
Believe me, my dear friend, he wrote, *tragedy has woven itself
through my life like a red ribbon.* He wrote:
Even the bright sky makes me sadder. All work is secret,

all times unreasonable. To love is to consent to distance.
I went back, to the dirt track through the Ravenscrag
Formation, its rose striations in cuts and erosions,
greasewood, sage and cactus prevailing on the upslope,

willow, cottonwood close to water, long bonebeds
of the Cretaceous and Paleocene, graves we worship
by digging at. I walked the margins of the Williston Basin
without knowing it; over sandstones, shale, muddy siltstone,

claystones, lateral sheets of braided river gravels, near lost
on the lignite alluvial plain within sight of uranium deposits
JNR Corp. has its eye on, and probably trespassing. Some people
are outfitted with odd and foolish habits. An unregulated

look. Has the devil any servant on earth so perfect
as the stranger? Who hears, always, dice thrown
on the outskirts, and whose cause is yet to be proven?
Things aren't meant to happen, yet they happen

nonetheless. I stayed in that country, travelled until dark
the first night of the Perseids while cloud massed
to the discernible horizon, and read it as a sign,
though it was no sign. Your leaving opened up a view

like that from the cliffs in their coarse conglomerate
sequence, out to where lines, the great circles, intersect.
Where symmetries radiate from a first principle and all opposites
are contained, no one thing taking precedence. That day,

the smell of rained-on grasses was narcotic, rising
from the ground in a mineral swarm. It was added to us,
our fire visible for miles, as late afternoon bent
to the rangeland and laid its shining weapons down.

Notes

In "Pathology of the Senses" are lines that include adapted definitions from *The Penguin Dictionary of Biology* (10th Ed. M. Thain and M. Hickman, ed. London: Penguin, 2000).

Lines from the fourth factory in "Four Factories" are quotes and paraphrases from Lakeside Packers recruitment literature and websites.

The italicized line in "Air Show" was the theme of the 2008 Canadian National Exhibition Air Show.

The Ludwig Wittgenstein quote in "Archive" is from *Remarks on Colour* (ed. G.E.M. Anscombe. Linda L. McAlister and Margarete Schattle, trans. Berkeley and Los Angeles: University of California Press, 1977).

Some lines in "Prayers for the Sick" are adapted from the Catholic *Prayers for the Sick.*

The epigraph for "Jesus Heals the Leopard" is from William Cowper's *The Task: A Poem in Six Books* (Philadelphia: Bennett and Walton, 1811).

In "Norway," the Knut Hamsun quote is from the opening lines of *Hunger* (Sigrid Undset, trans. Sverre Lyngstad, ed. New York: Penguin, 1998). The Eivind Groven tribute was delivered by Arne Nordheim on the occasion of Groven's 60th birthday in 1961. Also italicized are Norwegian proverbs, and a quote attributed to Vilhelm Bjerknes on the MacTutor History of Mathematics archive website (January, 2009. Created by John J. O'Connor and Edmund F. Robertson).

In "Postscript," the italicized lines are from Gauss's letters as quoted in Jane Muir's *Of Men and Numbers* (New York: Dodd, Mead & Co., 1961).

Acknowledgements

Earlier versions of some of these poems have appeared in *Arc*, *Brick*, *Exile*, *The Fiddlehead*, *Qwerty*, and *The Walrus*. My thanks to the editors of each.

I am grateful to the Canada Council for the Arts, Ontario Arts Council, and Toronto Arts Council for the financial assistance that allowed me to write this book.

Many thanks also to The Banff Centre for the Arts, University of New Brunswick, and Sage Hill Writing Experience for their support.

Thanks to Kevin Connolly, Michael Helm, and David Seymour for their encouragement and advice on drafts of poems. And especially to my editor, Ken Babstock, for his patience, intelligence, talent, and unfailing friendship.

To Lynn Henry and everyone at House of Anansi Press for their confidence in this project and work on its behalf. Also to Kitty Lewis at Brick Books for what she does and who she is.

To Garie and Ron Seymour, Jeff Seymour and Tracy Robertson, Rhea Seymour, Kirk and Sophie Layton for their affection and generosity.

And, always, to Howard and Hilda Solie, Craig Solie and Freya Brehaut, Dianne, Mike, Alison, and Jordan Brodie, for everything.

About the Author

KAREN SOLIE's first collection of poems, *Short Haul Engine*, won the Dorothy Livesay Poetry Prize and was shortlisted for the Griffin Poetry Prize, the ReLit Award, and the Gerald Lampert Memorial Award. Her second collection, *Modern and Normal*, was shortlisted for the Trillium Award for Poetry. Her poetry, fiction, nonfiction, and reviews have appeared in many magazines and journals. In 2007, Solie was one of the judges of the Griffin Poetry Prize. Solie is a native of Saskatchewan and now lives in Toronto.